*"If people would treat each other
with just a little common courtesy
and perhaps be more respectful of one another,
then there would be a lot less friction in the world."*

— Helga Walby

THE
DisGrruntled
EMPLOYEE'S
ULTIMATE
HANDBOOK

by Bryan Cahill

Canadian Cataloguing in Publication Data

Cahill, Bryan.
   The disgruntled employees' ultimate handbook

   ISBN 1-55212-474-6

   1. Violence in the workplace--Prevention. 2. Anger in the workplace. I. Title.
HF5549.E43C34 2000   658.4'73   C00-911103-4

TRAFFORD

This book was published *on-demand* in cooperation with Trafford Publishing.
On-demand publishing is a unique process and service of making a book available for retail sale to the public taking advantage of on-demand manufacturing and Internet marketing.
On-demand publishing includes promotions, retail sales, manufacturing, order fulfilment, accounting and collecting royalties on behalf of the author.

Suite 6E, 2333 Government St., Victoria, B.C. V8T 4P4, CANADA
Phone   250-383-6864   Toll-free   1-888-232-4444 (Canada & US)
Fax   250-383-6804   E-mail   sales@trafford.com
Web site   www.trafford.com   TRAFFORD IS A DIVISIONN OF TRAFFORD HOLDINGS LTD.
Trafford Catalogue #00-0139   www.trafford.com/robots/00-0139.html

10   9   8   7   6   5   4

This book was inspired by....

Well, they know who they are, there is no need to give them any credit now.

THANKS TO:
All the numerous Web sites that offer an invaluable insight into workplace violence, APBNEWS.COM, AMW.COM, USAToday.com, Honolulu's Starbulletin.com, Seattletimes .com, and all the various law enforcement agencies' Web sites.

SPECIAL THANKS TO:
Scruffy Duffy's, Kevin I., Kevin R., my family, Kirsten A., Sven W., Jim A., Tony R., Curtis S., Tony B., Eric S., Rick K., Steve H., Sherri S., Jennifer D., Rich B., Mark N., Kari R., Paul N., John V., Monte H., Rich R., Bill O., Mark F., Dennis G., the Miami connection Barbara K., the Key West Crew Gregg M., Gina D., Megan W., all the reference librarians at The New York Public Library, The Key West Public Library and anyone I met along the way that showed support for the book. Also all the professors I was fortunate enough to have: Prof. Lebow, Prof. Bennett, Prof. Bruno, Prof. Devitt, Prof. Terry, and of course my English professors, Dr. Blake and Karen.

A VERY SPECIAL THANKS TO:
God, for helping me get through all that, Jack Q., Dr. Gary M., Christopher S., and Helga W.

TABLE OF CONTENTS

Workplace violence. Documented cases with staggering statistics, initial procedures to possibly prevent workplace violence.

The documentation process, step-by-step guidelines to ensure proper documentation, chain of command, and your company's policies.

The procedures to follow when actually having to report any harassing behavior. The reasons people are reluctant to report any harassing behavior. The reverberation that may possibly be caused by reporting any harassing behavior.

When reporting any harassing behavior proves to be ineffective the procedures to follow next. Includes utilizing your chain of command, heightened awareness of your work surroundings, and the importance of familiarizing yourself thoroughly on all company policies.

Governmental agencies discussed more in depth and important recent law changes affecting the workplace. A complete and comprehensive listing of agencies to assist you, including EEOC, ADA, Department of Labor, Department of

Justice, listings for every situation including racial, veterans', women's, gay-related, etc., legal aid assistance, mental health facilities, and hotlines.

When the job is definitely gone, no chance for reemployment or any severance package. The importance of keeping it legal, no revenge, no sabotage, no vengeance, additional listings of worthy recognition.

Continuing procedures to follow to possibly prevent workplace violence, fact gathering, including effective listening, motivation, the difference between empathy and sympathy, the proper steps to actually terminate a DisGruntled Employee safely and legally and more importantly to ensure their 100% silence.

PREFACE

STOP. STOP IT. JUST STOP. Now take a deep breath, that's it. Calm down and just relax. Count from ten backward. Ten, nine, that's it, breathe deep. Eight, seven, exhale. Six, five, breathe deep. Four, three, exhale. Two, relax, breathe deep. One, exhale. That's it, just calm down. Take another deep breath. Go get a glass of cold water. Sit down and relax. Drink your water. Feel a little better now?

You are angry! How can you not be? Who in their right mind wouldn't be? When are they going to leave you be, to do your job in a harassment-free work environment? Managers, supervisors and bosses (hereafter m/s/b) can be so very ignorant in today's work force. Coworkers and colleagues can also be very mean spirited. One day they are smiling at you, the next day they are talking about you behind your back.

The work force is structured in such a way that we are all striving for the same goals in our careers. These goals range from the same job, the same raise, the same title, the same promotion, the same corner office, the same schedule, whatever the case may be. While competing in the rat race people have, since the beginning of time and will continue to do so until the end of civilization, perform unspeakable actions toward their coworkers. The people you spend the majority of your life with can commit extremely horrible, unethical, and in some cases illegal acts. It is just a fact of life that "backstabbing" takes place in almost every single company, corporation, organization, business, firm, etc., in the world.

There are numerous reasons for this type of behavior. People will disparage or discredit their coworker in an attempt to climb the abstract corporate ladder. Others may just want to fit in. They'll go along with the crowd, whatever the office gossip is, group mentality. Still others are just plain mean. The possibilities are endless for an explanation for these types of actions. Right now though you couldn't care less what their reasons are, all you know is that you can't take it any more, not one more minute! You want revenge, immediate sweet revenge. Instant gratification just isn't quick enough. You have been pushed one time too many and you are going to "show them."

Get a grip, breathe deep, or they do win. Whatever your idea of "show them" is, it is wrong, and you know that. Take another deep breath. You are not thinking rationally. You are letting your emotions take over. It is very easy for emotions to take over. You MUST control it, if not it could lead to irrational and/or erratic behavior. Once that happens there is no turning back and they do win. What you do in a momentary rage can ruin hundreds of lives and you know you really don't want to go and do all that. Why throw your life away? They are not worth it.

Take another deep breath. Realize that you are better than all this temporary turmoil. You are intelligent enough to know between right and wrong. You know violence is never the answer. They hired you after you have shown that you do posses a certain degree of intelligence and smarts. "Show them", legally, just how intelligent and smart you really are.

Breathe deep. Make yourself a nice hot cup of tea, decaf of course, maybe a nice darjeeling or mango chamomile, and sit down. Take the time to read or look over the book before you react or overreact. There are listings of over 100 different agencies to assist you with whatever you are dealing with. You can work through this. The very last thing you need to do right now is something stupid. You have dreams, hopes and goals like everybody else in the world; don't let anyone take that away from you ...

AUTHOR'S NOTE

Profile of a DisGruntled Employee

Anyone can be a DisGruntled Employee, yet not everyone is going to return to his or her current workplace or ex-workplace and go on a murderous rampage. In over 95% of all DisGruntled Employee workplace violence shooting cases, the suspect fits the same exact profile:

- WHITE MALE
- 35 YEARS OR OLDER
- HISTORY OF WORK-RELATED PROBLEMS
- HISTORY OF DRUG and/or ALCOHOL PROBLEMS
- HISTORY OF FAMILY/ RELATIONSHIP PROBLEMS

To avoid repetition and save space the masculine gender will be used throughout the book.

Chapter 1

THE JOB HUNT

Workplace violence has escalated to an alarming all-time high and will continue to do so until drastic measures are implemented. There are nearly 1,000 people killed and 1.5 million people assaulted in their workplace EACH year. Workplace violence crimes all have different contributing factors. These factors range from contact with the public, working alone or in small groups, late night work, security work guarding valuables, or any type of law enforcement work. The last contributing factor in workplace violence is working with the volatile person, the DisGruntled Employee.

Every company has some internal conflict. This book is focused on resolving internal conflict peacefully. If it cannot be resolved peacefully, then steps and procedures need to be taken to resolve the conflict legally. It is imperative to resolve all situations before they have a chance to escalate into a catastrophic occurrence. The most important reason is to prevent the devastating loss of any more valuable lives.

The Occupational Safety and Health Administration (OSHA) is a division under the Department of Labor. OSHA's statistics indicate that 1999 was the bloodiest year ever in workplace violence history. Early indication projects the year 2000 workplace violence statistics to surpass even those of 1999. There have been thousands of innocent people murdered or injured at their jobs. No one is immune from a DisGruntled Employee.

June 29, 2000/Seattle, WA – A top pathologist at the University of Washington Center was shot and killed by one of his resident physicians. Dr. Jian Chen murdered Dr. Rodger Haggitt. Dr. Chen became enraged that his contract would not be renewed therefore he would be losing his job soon.

May 25, 2000/Queens, NY – Five Wendy's employees

were murdered execution style. A former employee, who had been fired for stealing, and a cohort performed the massacre. John "Benji" Taylor, 36, and his accomplice entered the restaurant and asked to speak to the manager by name. Seven employees were rounded up in the basement office where the safe was kept. They had all been shot with two of them surviving. The murderers made off with $2000 and the restaurants security surveillance tapes.

May 22, 2000/Tacoma, WA – A worker at a construction site becomes enraged at his boss. The worker goes to his car and retrieves a gun. He then shoots his boss to death.

April 13, 2000/El Paso, TX – Two strippers, Arlene Prince, 20, and Marlene Dunan, 21, were arrested for killing their friend and coworking stripper Tishia Latina Holmes, 21. Arlene and Marlene became disgruntled and strangled Tishia. They got mad because, as they put it, "Tishia would always get to slide down the good pole."

March 17, 2000/Irving, TX – Robert Wayne Harris, 28, was fired from his job at Mi-T-Fine Car Wash. He returned three days later. He killed five ex-coworkers and took an undetermined amount of cash.

February 10, 2000/Wall Street, NY – A bomb is set off in the financial capital of the world. No arrest made yet. Spokesmen for the police department say that a DisGruntled Employee from one of the two brokerage houses in the area is a major suspect.

February 2, 2000/Jacksonville, FL – Tracy Moss, 26, killed his supervisor. Matthew Wells was shot and killed at Diversified Products Manufacturing where he and Tracy had worked. Hours before the shooting Tracy methodically suffocated his present girlfriend and then his ex-wife. He committed suicide shortly after shooting his supervisor.

January 27, 2000/Pembroke Pines, FL – Femesha Foster, 32, a valued Wal-Mart employee, put rat poison in her boss's soda. The entire act was recorded on the store's surveillance cameras. Femesha was charged with attempted murder.

January 10, 2000/Port St. Lucie, FL – Mario Bentancourt shoots to death his boss and coworker. He had been fired only minutes earlier. He went to his car and retrieved a gun. After the shooting he said to witnesses, "Yeah that's right, I shot them. They'll never ruin my day again." He is still on the run.

Happy New Millennium!

December 30, 1999/Tampa Bay, FL – A DisGruntled Employee of the Radisson Corporation Hotel chain went berserk, shoots and kills four coworkers and a woman as he escapes in her car.

December 8, 1999/Knoxville, TN – William D. Maines, 52, killed his ex-employer. William was an account manager who had been fired four weeks earlier for alleged numerous alcohol abuse infractions.

December 3, 1999 – Multi millionaire Edmund Safra was murdered. He was one of the wealthiest men in the world. He employed a complete security staff including around-the-clock bodyguards. It was discovered, after three days of intensive thorough interrogation, that a DisGruntled Employee, Ted Maher, 41, a personal nurse of Mr. Safra's, had set the fire that killed his employer.

November 15, 1999/Philadelphia, PA – Natasha Arrington was a diner waitress who was not pleased with having to work the early shift. She threw menus at some customers and was discourteous to others. The manager reprimanded Natasha when she proceeded to fly into a rage. She stormed out of the restaurant shouting, "Bullets will fly." She returned later in the morning with her boyfriend, who shot the manager twice in the leg.

November 3, 1999/Seattle, WA – Kevin Cruz shot four people, two died and two survived. Kevin was employed at a shipyard. He tried to claim disability but was denied. He blamed his ex-employer, the shipyard, for his disability claim being rejected.

November 2, 1999/Honolulu, HI – Byran Uyesugi shot seven of his coworkers to death at their Xerox office. He was employed in the technical service division.

October 9, 1999/Elkins, WV – Jeffrey White killed Harry Simons. Harry's bullet-riddled body was discovered at a lumberyard where they both had worked. Just before the shooting the two were arguing over Beanie Babies, witnesses say.

October 8, 1999/Pontiac, MI – Police arrest Cornelius Cruz for the 1998 murder of his ex-manager, Shirley Lynn Elko. They both had worked together at a KFC. Cornelius was apprehended on his way to work at a different KFC.

September 29, 1999/Alexandria, VA – Terrell Johnson, 27, was a police civilian employee. She was a record keeper in a rage. She set the two fires that caused extensive damage to the police headquarters where she worked.

September 10, 1999/Union City, NJ – The doorman, Robert Williams, of a luxury high rise building, The Lenox, shot and killed his boss, Barry Segall, the landlord. The shooting took place after an argument over a shift change.

August 5, 1999/Pelham, AL – Alan Eugene Miller shot and killed two coworkers at his current job. He then drove to his ex-employer where he proceeded to kill an ex-coworker there.

August 4, 1999/Sault Ste. Marie, MI – Former newspaper courier, Nathan Hanna, 40, is convicted of gunning down an executive, Anthony Gillespie. Mr. Gillespie was an executive at *The Evening News of Sault Ste. Marie*. Nathan had been employed there as a newspaper courier. Nathan claimed that he "didn't want the route with all the hills" and that his ex-boss "was the antichrist."

July 29, 1999/Charlotte, NC – A worker at Watkins Motor Lines Truck Plant in West Charlotte shot a coworker to death then turned the gun on himself.

June 19, 1999/Norristown, PA – Dennis Czajkowski returns to his former place of employment, the Norristown State Hospital. He had been fired eight weeks earlier. He burst into the nursing station, fired shots, and took two nursing supervisors hostage. This started a three-day standoff. When it was all over Dennis had killed his supervisor, Carol Sue Kepner.

Once the problem employee quits or is fired the problem is not always gone. **It is quite often the case that the DisGruntled Employee returns to wreak havoc after he has been terminated.** NO PERSON, COMPANY, CORPORATION, ORGANIZATION, BUSINESS, FIRM, ETC., IS SAFE FROM A DERANGED DisGruntled Employee! These examples were taken over a twelve-month time period from June 1999 to June 2000 and are not all-inclusive.

There are thousands of other documented cases on the subject of DisGruntled Employees and workplace violence involving shootings, physical attacks, harassments, and threats. One of the worst events in workplace violence history dates back to August 20, 1986, in Edmond, OK. Pat Sherrill, 44, a postal worker killed fourteen coworkers, then himself. Other post office workplace violence shooting incidents include the rampages in Royal Oak, Michigan, Dearborn, Michigan, and Dana Point, California. The popular phrase "going postal" materialized after these tragic events.

People become disgruntled for a various number of reasons. Any outrageous behavior cannot be blamed solely on the problems of society, yet at the same time it must be duly noted that the stress of modern-day life can at times be overwhelming. The dilemmas we face today as a society were rarely, if ever, heard of a mere generation ago. Crack, divorce rate over 50%, gun availability, school shootings, depletion of the ozone layer, designer drugs, huffing, car jacking, terrorist bombs on U.S. soil, more racial riots, rage in general. Not to say that these problems weren't happening in a few small isolated incidents perhaps somewhere. They were just nothing like the mess they have snowballed into in the last two decades of the twentieth century.

Recently discovered medical diseases are a current problem of societies' as well. AIDS, Lyme disease, herpes, Alzheimer's, mad cow disease, flesh-eating bacteria, E-coli outbreaks, melanoma, different forms of cancer, all these diseases have just recently made headlines. They may have been around and known about amongst the medical field but most were not even heard of by the general population before 1980.

Unfortunately, then there are hundreds of crimes and diseases already in existence. Plus various accidents happen daily with catastrophic results also. Taking this all into account, 100% of the entire work force has experienced some sort of emotional hardship. They could be from broken homes or going through divorces themselves. They could be victims of any number of crimes, or lost people dear to them. Regardless of the particulars everyone entering the work force has experienced some sort of emotional hardship. It just doesn't happen that someone lives the perfect life, divorce-free, disease-free, accident-free, death-free, crime-free, etc.. Some people just happen to enter the work force with more emotional hardship experiences than others.

The majority of society is capable of effective grieving. For most, time helps in the grieving process. For others, the help of a therapist or maybe even a psychiatrist is needed. Time was, pre-1980s, a stereotypical, negative, stigma was attached to anyone who sought outside professional help. Today it is very common for a person to get some sort of counseling, whether it is group or individual. Whatever it takes for a person to get on with his life and continue being a law-abiding productive member of society should be encouraged.

To recap Chapter 1

Violence in the workplace has escalated to an all-time high. Workplace violence will continue to grow unless drastic changes are made. These initial procedures could be as follows: extremely thorough background checks on all potential employees, a week-long orientation process of all new hires to instill the fact that harassment of any kind will not be tolerated, metal detectors at employee entrances, new laws passed or old ones amended. Employers can make sure that all lines of communication are open, ensure all employees have 100% mental coverage as part of their benefits package, or it could be something as simple as listening. Changes need to be implemented or this workplace violence trend will continue to rise.

Chapter 2

THE NEW JOB

People are generally shy and do not say too much, maybe even a little timid, during their first few days at a new company. They hardly reveal anything about their personal life and that is the way it should remain, low key. It is too often the case that people get comfortable with their coworkers and then they become too self-revealing. They just want to fit in. Nobody wants to be labeled unfriendly or standoffish. Even worse, nobody wants gossip, rumors, accusations, etc., made against them. Nor do they ever want the stigma of being labeled crazy, touched, head case, sick boy, etc., When a person does get that image, their reputation is over at least in that particular workplace. This person's credibility can never be restored.

If you have the feeling that you are being bullied, harassed, picked on, made fun of, singled out, hurt in any manner for any reason, well then you probably are. No one could possibly know any better than you what you are feeling. The very first time you get an uncomfortable feeling from a coworker, supervisor, manager, or any other employee you must document it. Hopefully it will turn out to be nothing. People can, at times, overstep their personal boundaries and be very obnoxious, without even realizing they are being offensive. In most case scenarios the incident will turn out to be nothing and be completely forgotten. That would be the best thing possible. No one looks forward to any confrontation at his job. Life already offers ample levels of stress as it is; not to mention that the actual work (the reason why you were hired) is hard enough without having a conflict with a colleague.

Crime statistics indicate that an overwhelming number of workplace violence cases occur after recurring harassment incidents that were allowed to continue to escalate.

For this very reason, it is important that you document everything. It may assist in avoiding conflict later. Proper documentation is essential and required. Any time you are made to feel uneasy document it. Be very discreet about it. Keep a separate notebook. Make it very legible and easily understandable.

How exactly does one properly document everything? Any time an incident occurs, anything no matter how minor, write out what just happened. Scribble it down on any paper, a Post-It, scratch paper, an envelope, a napkin, anything for the time being. Write it down while it is still fresh in your mind. Rewrite it later at home in your separate notebook, when you have the time.

These four questions MUST be answered to ensure proper documentation: WHO, WHAT, WHERE, and WHEN.

WHO? Who did what? (offenders, harassers). Who was there? Who saw what? (supervisors, managers, other employees, potential witnesses)

WHAT? What actually happened? What is making you feel uncomfortable/ harassed? Is it a nasty comment, a dirty look, nasty cartoons drawn at your expense placed throughout your work area, personal belongings being messed with, schedule changes without notification, threats of physical violence, a physical attack, etc., any number of things. Whatever the incident is, no matter how minor it may appear at the time, document it. Try to include quotes of what was said.

IF YOU ARE EVER PHYSICALLY ATTACKED IN THE WORKPLACE PROCEED TO THE NEAREST PHONE AND DIAL 911. YOUR PLACE OF EMPLOYMENT HAS FAILED TO PROVIDE FOR YOUR SAFETY AND YOU NEED IMMEDIATE LEGAL INTERVENTION.

WHERE? Very self-explanatory, where did the incident take place? (i.e., employee entrance, employee locker room, office, cafeteria, desk, lobby, board room, reception area, kitchen, elevator, storage area, employee parking lot, etc.) Be very detailed about where the infraction occurred.

WHEN? Again very self-explanatory, be very specific, time, am or pm, day AND date including the year.

While you are documenting every incident you MUST get a copy of your company's policies. Most corporations and any good company has a set of procedures and protocol in which they implement into their own policies. During an orientation of the company a copy of the company's policies should have been given to you. Locate it. If you did not get one or you lost yours get another copy. Be very subtle about obtaining one. No one ever seeks a copy of their company's policies when things are going great. It is only when there is trouble when anyone wants to see their company's policies. If you are asking around for a copy of your company's policies, questions will be raised so be very discreet.

Familiarize yourself with all the company's policies, in particular the company's policy on harassment. For the most part all corporations have basically the same harassment policy, regardless of the actual wording. They generally are brief and stress the fact that harassment of any kind will not be tolerated throughout the company. If the company's harassment policy is written correctly is should be very inclusive and cover nearly all possibilities. It is important that you become familiar with your own company's particular harassment policy.

Also learn your chain of command. Who is your immediate supervisor? What is his/her title? Who is their supervisor? What is their title? Who is the CEO? Who is on the executive committee, especially the Director of Human Resources? Who is the owner? Who is the general manager? Who is actually running the place?

If the harassment continues perhaps some degree of

intervention will be necessary. You will have to be ready then. You cannot be left standing there raging something like "Uh, ten days ago, no, I mean two weeks ago... yeah, it was two weeks ago Tuesday, he told me he was going to beat me up, or did he say kick my ass? Or well... whatever. Kyle was there and so was James, I think. It happened, uh, after lunch around 1:15 pm— No, no, uh, 2:00! Yeah, that's it, it was closer to two."

You would be perceived as a babbling buffoon.

The reason you have documented everything is so that you can show a pattern of harassing behavior. You need to be prepared. You need to rationally state your case. An example would be "On Friday, January 13, 1999, at 2:12 am (when) Sam Smith (who) approached me aggressively (what) at the water cooler in the break room (where) and growled, "Just wait, pal... What time you get off?" and stormed away (more what, physically and verbally threatening). Robert Alguire and Delia Rossi (more who) were in the break room at the time of the occurrence."

To recap chapter 2

Document any harassing incident, obtain a copy of your company's policies and learn your chain of command. You very well may have been harassed, threatened, physically attacked, etc., but unless the incident is properly documented it will be as if it never happened.

Chapter 3

THE NEXT LEVEL

We are all told by our parents and teachers "Don't be a tattletale" as we are growing up. Throughout school we learn the word *fink* and the negative connotation that goes along with the term. The rat stigma is the last thing anyone wants to be labeled when they enter the work force. Nobody knows how long their new job at any company will last when they just start. Most people have the same thoughts running through their minds. "Will it work out? Will I retire with this company? Will I like it enough to last a month?" No one ever can tell. For these two reasons, the rat distinction and the uncertainty of the longevity of one's tenure at a company, a person may be reluctant to come forward with any allegations against a colleague. No one looks forward to creating any problems in their workplace.

This is all fine and good but there comes a time when you have no choice, you must do something. Once you realize that the harassment/offending incidents are not going to stop without intervention and you have at least a few incidents documented, then contact your immediate supervisor as soon as possible. It is critical that you follow your particular company's policy. This is why it is extremely crucial that you have proper documentation and that you know your chain of command. Your first step would be to contact your immediate supervisor. Make an appointment with this person. If this person is your immediate supervisor, there is no acceptable reason that he or she cannot take ten minutes out of his or her day to sit down somewhere privately and speak with you.

Do not attempt to "catch them" between meetings or after lunch, in the hallway, etc., for a brief moment. No way, forget it, it won't work. Someone walking by could possibly distract the m/s/b, you then could forget something important that you needed to say. The person(s) you are alleging harassment from may see you talking to the m/s/b you then could lose your train of thought. Any number of outside occurrences may happen. You want their 100% complete uninterrupted attention for ten minutes at a minimum. There is no acceptable reason why your immediate supervisor cannot grant you at least that much time.

Continue documenting everything. Now it becomes more critical than ever. The last thing you could have possibly wanted to do is actually report a coworker. You obviously feel it is the only option left. Call your immediate supervisor. Document it. What time, date did you call? Did you talk to him/her? Receptionist? Answering machine? Voice mail? What was the result? Document when your call was returned. What was said? Is a meeting arranged, and if no, why not?

The meeting, document it of course, who, what, where, when. Make completely sure that you are clear on the employer's course of action. What are they going to do about this situation? The employer should then talk to the offending employee(s). The offender(s) may just be oblivious to the fact that they are being offensive, they may think that they are merely being comical. Once they are made aware of the situation it could be resolved right there. That would be the best-case scenario that it just ends right there and then. You felt offended, you got it off your chest, and now it is all resolved.

Unfortunately, that doesn't happen quite enough. There could be after thoughts on everybody's part. If the situation is not rectified then, the employee may feel let down and think the supervisor is incompetent. The m/s/b(s) in turn could now have the thoughts of "Who is this person launching complaints and documenting everything? Do we have a problem employee?" The offender(s) could have the thoughts: "What?!!! He said what about me/us? Who does this person think they are telling on?" For all these reasons people just won't come forward. People are basically the same. Regardless of race, sex, religion, they all want the same things. They want to fit in with society. They want to make a good living so they can provide for their families and children. No one ever wants to be labeled a "rat" or "problem employee," so when there is a situation people tend to just endure the torment. You do not have to endure it. You are legally entitled to a harassment free work environment.

Enduring it will not work. You may be able to take it for a while but over time you will erupt. It will happen, maybe eight months maybe six years, but it will occur.

If you do not report it and you are continually harassed it could very well lead to an incident in which you overreact. If you do blow up and lose your cool then you completely lose your credibility from that moment on. You then start to be perceived in a very negative way, i.e., erratic, uncontrollable, abusive, raging lunatic, threatening, menacing, etc., you will never be taken seriously ever again. One minor overreaction incident and you will be the one labeled "problem employee" immediately.

You want to avoid that at all cost. You must maintain your composure and remain rational. If you do get upset and have an incident in which you overreact, the offenders can now use it against you. It may have happened only once but that is all it takes. You might raise your voice, swear, or even spout out something in a momentary rage that you could never possibly mean. The harasser(s), the very same person(s) who have been the source of the problem, can turn it around and report you to their immediate supervisor. They can now report something similar to this: "Look how he acts, he screams and swears and is very intimidating. He is prone to outburst. I am in fear of my safety."

They can get away with saying anything at all at this point maybe even sprinkle in a few lies. Your credibility vanished when you overreacted.

Once charges are launched against you, your problems have just increased. You are now put on the defensive on a whole different level. You have become the accused and you are fighting an uphill battle. Anything you say will be disregarded. Even if you were to now produce extensive documentation of a series of harassing incidents, none of it will be taken into account. Every m/s/b will be asking the same question: "Why didn't you tell any of us about the harassment incidents in the past? It seems very coincidental that now you want to file formal harassment charges, only after a valid complaint has been launched against you." Your credibility has vanished never to be restored.

For this very reason it is so very important that you report it. Forget what you've been taught in grade school about "Don't be a tattletale"; if someone is harassing you report it.

There is cause and effect. You reported an offender, the cause. Now their reaction is the effect. There are two different effects that can happen. First effect is that the harassment just ends right then and there. That would be the best-case scenario. The second effect is that the offenders can get perturbed now that you've brought up a grievance against them. The trouble can start to escalate. More harassment incidents could start to follow and the "rat, fink, tattletale" discredit could start to emerge. This is all further harassment. You need to then repeat the procedure. Continue to document everything. Make another appointment with your immediate supervisor after a few more documented incidents.

You have tried to dissolve the situation by going to your immediate supervisor but the situation has escalated. You no longer find pleasure in your job. You may even experience the feeling of trepidation with all the continued harassment. You must continue up the chain of command until you reach some sort of resolution. The more m/s/b(s) that you contact the greater the risk you run of the "problem employee" dishonor. They can now start to build a constructive discharge case against you. Continue to document everything, every supervisor you ever speak to, every harassing incident. Did the m/s/b(s) take the course of action that they said they were going to do in the last meeting? What was the outcome of their speaking to the offender? Is it ever going to stop?

Two ways to avoid the problem employee stigma are, first, do not allow a situation to escalate in which you could possibly have an overreaction incident, report it before it builds up; second, when reporting an incident speak rationally. Exercise the most rational behavior possible when you finally get your meeting(s) with the m/s/b(s).

Speak calmly, concisely, and slowly. Do not rush any of your thoughts. In a lot of cases this will be the very first contact you have with the higher-ups in the chain of command or in the executive committee. You may have seen each other around or even said hello at a company gathering or whatever, but this will be the very first time that you ever sit down together. You better believe that they have been briefed on you and your case. The whole thing about first impressions is true. If you go into your meeting rational and present your case in a respectable manner then there is a good chance the whole situation can still be peacefully resolved. On the other hand if you go into your meeting unprepared, speaking loudly, very fast, emotional, erratic, accusing, finger pointing, etc. without any proper documentation, then you will be perceived as a problem employee.

To recap Chapter 3

Report it. Do not allow any problems to build up. Report it in the most extremely professional manner possible. Fear of being labeled a rat, fink, problem employee, etc., or fear of further harassment, retaliation, keeps people from reporting harassing incidents. This is when the situation then has a chance to escalate to unsafe levels.

Chapter 4

A TURN FOR THE WORSE

The harassment continues. It appears to you that after reporting the incident to your immediate supervisor that either nothing was said or done to the offender(s) or if there was, it was ineffective. You must continue to document everything while you climb the chain of command. This time you must go to your supervisor's supervisor. Repeat the procedure, make an appointment with this person, document it, etc.

The risk in utilizing your chain of command is that the m/s/b(s) can form a bond with each other, a clique. Giving them the benefit of the doubt, after all they were able to achieve their current positions; the m/s/b(s) do possess the capability of being fair and just. This is exactly what you are hoping for. In other cases they could be close friends that may happen to do weekend activities together. Again, if you are unprepared or you speak irrationally you will be perceived in a negative image. The problem employee stigma will be etched in stone.

Every company that happens to employ a problem worker only wants one thing: that the disruptive individual be terminated. If you get deemed a problem employee they want you gone, that simple. The m/s/b(s) are now documenting each and every incident that can be used at a later date against you. Were you late one minute?; Did you leave a little early?; How long were you on break?; Were you out of uniform?; Were you out of line?; etc. Every single move you make is being scrutinized and recorded. They are continuing to establish their constructive discharge case against you now. They are documenting everything against you. You do the exact same thing and beat them at their own game by documenting everything you see.

Note everything. Count the number of employees if possible. Are there an adequate number of minorities represented? Are there enough women present? Are the working conditions safe? Are the stairwells up to code, lit well with handrails on both sides? Are the fire exits free of clutter or are they blocked? Are the cleaning chemicals being stored properly? What about chemicals for the copy machine? Is there recycling done throughout the building? Anything you see which you may think violates any laws, whatever it is, document it. Is it a restaurant? How about cleanliness? Is the chef wearing a hair net? Are the food handlers their washing hands? Are the employees legal aliens with proper working papers? Health code standards up to par? Is it a retail establishment? Are all the sales being conducted properly? Over the counter and properly recorded? Or are any of the sales being made out the back door "tax exempt"? Is it a movie theater? Are the child labor laws being adhered to for the ushers and counter workers? Is it a hospital? Are the interns given the legally required time off to adequately rest or are they overworked? Is it a construction site? Are all safety measures implemented? Is the scaffolding in place properly? Are there corners being cut anywhere? The possibilities are endless...

No illegality is too minute to take notice of.

Continue to note everything as you locate a copy of your company's policies, at this point in time, it is imperative. It is extremely crucial that you have a copy of your company's policies. If you still do not have a copy get one. Ask immediately in the Human Resources or personnel department. Document it. Who did you ask? What was their response? Were they helpful or hindering? etc.

The task of documenting everything may be a bit excessive albeit necessary.

The importance of having a copy of the company's policies is so that you can ensure that the m/s/b(s) are adhering to the company policies as well. M/s/b(s) are also employees of the company. They must follow company rules and regulations just like the workers that they are hired to oversee. The fact that they may have a title does not put them above practices and procedures.

The reason that you need to read and learn your company's policies is so that you will know when the policies are being violated and/or broken. For example, most companies have a policy against gambling in the workplace. The policy is usually very specific to include football pools, betting cards, to outright wagers. Regardless of the no gambling policy, at the company, football pools, especially for the Superbowl, do take place in a lot of offices nationwide. A lot of the time the m/s/b(s) play right along, getting involved in the pool by choosing a few boxes themselves. Document it. If possible try to get a copy of the football pool with the actual m/s/b(s)' initials on it.

The fact that a m/s/b plays along in a football pool may appear minute, nonetheless it is a company policy that the m/s/b decides to not follow. These people make decisions daily affecting hundreds of employees' lives. It would be sheer abuse of power if these people were left alone to choose which particular policies that they will adhere to and which ones that they won't. In addition to a company policy being broken, gambling and football pools are still illegal in many states.

Continue to take notice of, and make a note on every single item, infraction, incident. At a later date in time you may have to seek legal counsel, or approach any number of agencies including OSHA, IRS, EEOC, Department of Labor, Human Rights Commission, ACLU, NYCLU, ADA, Building, Fire, Health Inspectors, etc., and you always want to be, and must be, well prepared with as much proper documentation as possible.

To recap Chapter 4

Utilize your chain of command in your quest for a harassment-free work environment. Note everything. If you are
not getting the satisfaction that you require in house, perhaps maybe an outside agency's intervention at a later date
will be of some assistance. And get that copy of your company's policies.

Chapter 5

YOU'RE FIRED!!!

It has become abundantly clear that your company is moving for your termination. You have either been told to leave, or you are escorted from the building, or you could flat out be denied entrance into your workplace. Whatever the case may be they are firing you. You are probably very upset, who wouldn't be, getting fired and all? You must remain rational. First of all think it over. Do you really want your job back? Was the pay what you needed/wanted? Were the benefits as good as you thought they would be? How was the vacation time? How about time off to be with the family, was it adequate? How was the commute? How were the working conditions? How were the coworkers? Take every factor in your work environment into consideration. In some cases, getting fired could be the best thing possible, although you could not possibly recognize it, at the present time.

Do you really want your job back? Or is your pride hurt? If you are sure that you want it back, then do everything possible to try to get it back. There are no guarantees that you will regain your job, but there is help out there. Be ready to roll up your sleeves and do battle (figuratively). Best of luck and sock it to them. Remember be calm, speak rational, and most importantly be well prepared with all your proper documentation.

This book will provide you with a listing of over 100 different agencies to assist you in getting started. You will need to do some research work on your own, as every case is different. Next you will need a crash course on federal agencies and recent law changes.

E.E.O.C. Board – After the civil rights act, the Equal Employment Opportunity Commission was founded in 1964.

The E.E.O.C.'s charter is to fight discrimination in all aspects of employment. Most discrimination cases fall under these guidelines, including natural origin, religion, disability, color, sex, and race. These are all covered by this agency. **N.L.R.B.** stands for the United States National Labor Relations Board. The board was created in 1935 to enforce the National Labor Relations Act. Contact this agency for any union related issues.

OSHA, as stated earlier, is an acronym for Occupational Safety & Health Administration, a division under the United States Department of Labor, which was established in 1970. If the safety and/or health of you and/or your coworkers is in jeopardy, at your workplace, this is the federal agency to contact. OSHA has three main purposes: to save lives, prevent injuries, and protect the health of the American worker.

Four laws that brought about some important changes in the work place throughout the 1990s were an environmental law, a disability law, a family leave act, and a veterans' law.

Environmental law – Mandatory recycling in all buildings and offices of all glass, plastic, paper, cans, cardboard, etc., If a company refuses to comply, it risks hefty fines.

Americans with Disabilities Act of 1990 – Every business or company, with fifteen or more employees, now must be ADA compliant and possess the ability to accommodate employees who are physically challenged.

Family and Medical Leave Act of 1993 – This law allows for qualified employees (immediate family members) up to twelve weeks of unpaid job protected leave with health benefits per year.

The Veterans Employment Opportunities Act of 1998 – Veterans now have access to federal jobs that might have been off limits to them in the past.

As stated prior, 1999 was the bloodiest year ever in workplace violence history, with over 1,000 people killed in their workplace. Is there anything being done about it?

DEPARTMENT OF LABOR – OCCUPATIONAL SAFETY AND HEALTH ADMINISTATIONS' Web site: http://www.Osha.gov/oshinfo/priorities/violence.html

Kind of ironic that "priorities" appears in there, look to page two of four half way down, under "Current Status." Or you can look up the public law at Section 5(a)(1) of the OSHA Act, or P.L. 91–596 (the "General Duty Clause")

Currently there are no federal laws or regulations requiring employers to implement any sort of workplace violence prevention programs. The United States government leaves it up to the sole discretion of the individual company. The executives of that company decide on whether or not they will implement any sort of workplace violence prevention programs. "Commitment to encourage" is the way it is phrased in the actual law. There is a general duty clause of 1970, but it's just too general and does not even mention workplace violence.

Leaving the decision up to the employer to implement a workplace violence prevention program proves to be ineffective. Big business's bottom line is money and implementing any sort of workplace violence prevention programs would be costly, time consuming, and not even required by law, so why bother? The general duty clause of some thirty years ago appears a bit outdated (especially considering gun availability).

Perhaps a new law needs to be added that would be very specific on the subject of workplace violence. It would REQUIRE employers to implement a workplace violence prevention program throughout their own company.

Another law that must be duly noted is the National Whistleblower Act. Certain provisions were added in 1986. The amendments made it easier for whistleblowers to benefit from their actions. A slight change in the law has made it extremely lucrative to blow the whistle. As a result, the added amendment to the law has assisted the United States Government to recover more than three billion dollars to date. A huge reward is offered, it ranges from 15 to 30% of any monies won in a settlement. For instance, the company that just ruined your life, your ex-employer, happens to evade millions of dollars in taxes and you have proof positive, reported to the appropriate agencies (National Whistleblowers Organization, IRS, state and city comptroller). Times the 15 to 30% reward, equals your retirement. Recent recoveries include $375 million from National Medical Center. Beverly Enterprises, Inc., paid $170 million in fines. Chevron paid $87 million. Olsten paid $40 million. Mobil paid, etc.

To recap Chapter 5

If you feel your termination is based on a discriminating factor in any manner, whether it be a disability, sexual orientation, women's issues, racial issues, veterans' rights, religion, etc., whatever the discriminating factor may be, the first agencies to contact would be: THE DEPARTMENT OF LABOR, THE DEPARTMENT OF JUSTICE, EEOC, ACLU, CIVIL RIGHTS COMMISSION in your area, YOUR CITY'S HUMAN RIGHTS COMMISSION, and YOUR CITY'S LEGAL AID SOCIETY.

You will be supplied with the appropriate information that you will need. You must also do some research work for yourself. It would not be feasible to publish the millions of phone numbers of every agency in every city and state. You will be given the NAMES of the agencies to contact in your area. Each scenario will be different so it is extremely crucial that you research your own particular case. Your local library offers an excellent source of information, as does the Internet or even your local phone book. The city of New York was used as an example as it is the largest.

GOVERNMENTAL AGENCIES
EQUAL EMPLOYMENT OPPORTUNITY COMMISSION

EEOC
1801 L STREET NW
WASHINGTON DC 20507
202-663-4494 TDD
WWW.EEOC.GOV/ (no spaces)
1-800-669-3362
1-800-800-3302 TDD

EEOC
255 E. TEMPLE 4TH FLOOR
LOS ANGELES, CA. 90012
213-894-1000
213-894-1121 TDD

EEOC
7 WORLD TRADE CENTER 18TH FLOOR
NEW YORK, N.Y. 10048-0948
212-748-8500
212-748-8399 TDD
1-800-669-4000

EEOC
1 BISCAYNE TOWER 2 SOUTH BISCAYNE
BLVD. SUITE 2700
MIAMI, FLA. 33131
305-536-4491
305-536-5721 TDD

OCCUPATIONAL SAFETY & HEALTH ADMINISRATION

U.S. DEPT. OF LABOR / OSHA
200 CONSTITUTION AVE.
WASHINGTON, D.C. 20210
202-693-2000

U.S. DEPT. OF LABOR / OSHA
201 VARICK STREET ROOM 670
NEW YORK, N.Y. 10014
212-337-2371 FAX

U.S. DEPT. OF LABOR / OSHA
8040 PETERS RD. BLDG. H-100
FORT LAUDERDALE, FLA. 33324
954-424-0242
954-424-3073 FAX

U.S.DEPT. OF LABOR / OSHA
71 STEVENSON STREET ROOM 420
SAN FRANCISCO, CA. 94105
415-975-4310
415-975-4319 FAX

IN CASE OF OSHA RELATED EMERGENCY CALL 1-800-321-OSHA

UNITED STATES NATIONAL LABOR RELATIONS BOARD

U.S.N.L.R.B.
1099 14ᵀᴴ STREET
WASHINGTON, D.C.
20570-0001
202-273-1991

U.S.N.L.R.B.
51 S.W. FIRST Ave.
FEDERAL BLDG. ROOM 565
MIAMI, FLA 33130-1608
305-536-5391
305-536-5320 FAX

U.S.N.L.R.B.
26 FEDERAL PLAZA
JACOB JAVITS BLDG. ROOM 3614
NEW YORK, N.Y. 10278-0104
REGIONAL DIRECTOR:
DANIEL SILVERMAN
212-264-0300
212-264-8427 FAX

U.S.N.L.R.B.
615 EAST HOUSTON STR. ROOM 565
SAN ANTONIO, TX 78205-2040
210-472-6140
210-472-6143 FAX

PEOPLE WITH DISABILITIES

THE PRESIDENTS' COMMITTEE ON
EMPLOYMENT OF PEOPLE
 WITH DISABILITIES
1331 F Str. N.W. 3ᴿᴰ Floor
Washington, D.C. 20004-1107
202-376-6200
202-376-6205
202-376-6219

OFFICE OF THE AMERICANS
WITH DISABILITIES ACT

U.S. Dept. of Justice
P.O.Box 66118
Washington, D.C. 20035-6118
202-514-0301
202-514-0318 TDD
202-514-0383 TDD
1-800-526-7234

N.Y. STATE ADVOCATE FOR PERSONS WITH DISABILITIES
1 Empire State Plaza Suite 1001
ALBANY, NEW YORK, 12223
518-473-4129

JOB ACCOMMODATIONS NETWORK
1-800-526-7234

DISABILITY LEGAL RESOURCES
1-800-466-4232

UNITED STATES DEPARTMENT OF LABOR

U.S. Dept. of Labor
Office of Public Affairs
200 Constitution Ave. N.W.
Room S-1032
Washington, D.C. 20210
202-693-4650

U.S. Dept. of Labor
Office of Public Affairs
1371 Peachtree Street. N.E.
Room 317
Atlanta, Ga. 30367
404-562-2080

U.S. Dept. of Labor
Office of Public Affairs
201 Varick Str. Room 605
New York, N.Y. 10014
212-337-2319

U.S. Dept. of Labor
Office of Public Affairs
71 Stevenson Str. Suite 1035
San Francisco, Ca. 94105
415-975-4740

U.S. Dept of Labor
WB Office of Public Affairs
200 Constitution Ave. N.W.
ROOM S-311
Washington, D.C. 20210
202-219-6652
WOMENS' BUREAU

U.S. Dept of Labor
Vets. Office of Public Affairs
200 Constitution Ave. N.W.
ROOM S-1310 A
Washington, D.C. 20210
202-219-5573
VETERANS' BUREAU

Most states still do not mandate **GAY RIGHTS LAWS.** Contact these agencies for assistance.

City Commission on Human Rights
40 Rector Street 9th floor
New York, N.Y. 10006
212-306-7500 Main
212-306-7530 Phone

National Gay & Lesbian Task Force
1700 Kalorama Rd. N.W.
Washington, D.C. 20009-2624
202-332-6483
202-332-6219 TDD

National Gay & Lesbian Task Force
121 West 27th Street Suite 501
New York, N.Y. 10001
212-604-9830

National Gay & Lesbian Task Force
1151 Massachusetts Avenue
Cambridge, Ma. 02138
617-492-6393 Phone
617-492-0175 Fax

LAMBDA- Legal Services
120 Wall Street Suite 1500
New York, N.Y. 10005
212-809-8585 Phone
212-809-0055 Fax

LAMBDA-Legal Services
6030 Wilshire Blvd.
Los Angeles, Ca. 90036-3617
323-937-2728 Phone
323-937-0601

Empire State Pride Agenda
212-627-0305

Anti-Violence Project
212-714-1184

CONSTITUTIONAL RIGHTS / BILL OF RIGHTS AGENCIES

Center for Constitutional Rights
666 Broadway 7th Floor
New York, N.Y. 10012
email CCR@igc.apc.org

American Civil Liberties Union (ACLU)
125 Broad Street 18th Floor
New York, N.Y. 10004
212-549-2500

New York Civil Liberties Union
125 Broad Street 17th Floor
New York, N.Y. 10004
212-344-3005
Exec. Director: Norman Siegel

ACLU of Southern California
1616 Beverly Boulevard
Los Angeles, CA. 90026
213-977-9500

CIVIL RIGHTS COMMISSIONS

Civil Rights Commission
61 Forsyth Street S.W.
Atlanta, Ga. 30303
Bobby D. Doctor, Director
404-562-7000

Civil Rights Commission
Suite 410
55 West Monroe Street
Chicago, Illinois 60603
Constance Davis, Director
312-353-8311

Civil Rights Commission
Suite 908
400 State Avenue
Kansas City, Kansas 66101
Melvin L. Jenkins, Director
913-551-1400

Civil Rights Commission
Suite 710
1700 Broadway
Denver, Co. 80290
John F. Dulles, Director
303-866-1040

Civil Rights Commission
Suite 810
3660 Wilshire Blvd.
Los Angeles, Ca.90010
Philip Montez, Director
213-894-3437

For all **WOMEN'S RELATED ISSUES** contact these agencies also:

9 to 5, National Association
of Working Women
614 Superior Ave. NW
Cleveland, Ohio 44113
1-800-522-0925

Women's Rights At Work
1-800-979-7765
1-800-WRW-PROJ

NOW Legal Defense Fund
395 Hudson Street
New York, N.Y. 10014
212-925-6635 Phone
212-226-1066 Fax

Women's Health Issues
301-827-0350

Equal Rights Advocates
1663 Mission Street
San Francisco, Ca. 94103
415-621-0505

NorthWest Women's Law Center
119 South Main Street Suite 330
Seattle, Washington 98104
206-682-9552
206-621-7691

U.S. Dept of Labor
WB Office of Public Affairs
200 Constitution Ave. N.W.
ROOM S-311
Washington, D.C. 20210
202-219-6652

US Dept. of Labor
Women's Bureau
New York, N.Y.
212-337-2389

Contact **THE DEPARTMENT OF VETERAN'S AFFAIRS** for all Veterans' related issues. The same 1-800-827-1000 phone number is used for all offices.

Department of Veterans Affairs HQ
810 Vermont Ave. N.W.
Washington, D.C. 20420
202-273-5400

Department of Veterans Affairs
245 West Houston Street
New York, N.Y. 10014

Department of Veterans Affairs
915 Second Avenue
Seattle, WA. 98174-1060

Department of Veterans Affairs
John F. Kennedy Bldg.-Room 1265
Boston, MA. 02203-0393

Department of Veterans Affairs
Federal Bldg.
11000 Wilshire Blvd.
Los Angeles, Ca. 90024

Department of Veterans Affairs
1600 E. Woodrow Wilson Ave.
Jackson, MS. 39216

Veterans' Employment & Training
201 Varick Street
New York, NY. 212-337-2211

LEGAL AGENCIES

Contact your local Legal Aid Society for referrals on free or sliding scale lawyers. Contact your local Bar Association for full fee attorneys.

Legal Aid Society of Los Angeles
Central Office
1550 West Eighth Street
Los Angeles, CA. 90017
213-487-7609

L.A.S. of L.A.-East Office
5228 East Whittier Blvd.
Los Angeles, CA. 90022
213-266-6550

L.A.S. of L.A.-Santa Monica Office
612 Colorado Ave. Suite 107-A
Santa Monica, CA. 90401
310-581-3300

L.A.S. of L.A.-South Central Office
8601 South Broadway
Los Angeles, CA. 90003
213-971-4102

L.A.S. of L.A.-West Office
1102 South Crenshaw Blvd., 1st Fl.
Los Angeles, CA. 90019
213-964-7600

Boston Lawyers
Committee for Civil Rights
294 Washington Street
Boston, MA. 02108
617-482-1145

Atlanta Legal Aid Society
151 Spring Street N.W.
Atlanta, GA. 30303
404-524-5811

Community Legal Services
305 South Second Avenue
P.O. Box 21538
Phoenix, AZ. 85036
602-258-3434
1-800-852-9075

Alaska Legal Service Corp.
1016 West Sixth Ave. Suite 200
Anchorage, Alaska 99051
907-276-6282

Pine Tree Legal Services
88 Federal Street
P.O. Box 547
Portland, Maine 04112
207-774-4753

Central Florida Legal Services
128-A Orange Ave.
Daytona Beach, FLA. 32114
904-255-6573
1-800-329-6573

Legal Aid Society of Wichita
North Empire Suite 500
Wichita, KS. 67202-2515
316-265-9681

Legal Defense & Education Fund
355 Hudson Street
New York, NY. 10014
212-925-6635

Legal Aid Society of New York
90 Church Street
New York, NY 10007
212-577-3300

ADDITIONAL AGENCIES OF WORTHY RECOGNITION

American Federation of Labor &
Congress of Industrial Organization
AFL-CIO
815 16th Street. N.W.
Washington, D.C. 20006
202-637-5000

National Whistleblowers Center
3238 P Street N.W.
Washington, D.C. 20007
202-342-1902
202-342-1904 Fax
202-342-6984 Fax
Email: Whistle@Whistleblowers.Org

Asian-American Legal Defense Fund
99 Hudson Street
New York, NY 10013-2815
212-966-5932

Puerto Rican Legal Defense Fund
99 Hudson Steet
New York, N.Y. 10014
212-219-3360

NAACP
144 West 125th Street
New York, N.Y. 10027
212-666-9740

Affirmative Action
Employment Discrimination
212-264-7742

Child Labor Hotline 1-800-959-3652

Department of Fair Employment
455 Golden Gate Ave. # 7600
San Francisco, CA. 94102
1-800-884-1684

Workers Compensation Claims
202-742-0702

Wage Discrimination 1-800-827-5335

MENTAL HEALTH ORGANIZATIONS

New York City Department of Mental Health   1-800-527-7474
Mental Health New York City   212- 442-5000
Mental Health Counseling Hotline   212-734-5876
Mental Health referrals   212-219-5600
Mental Health Information   212-219-5599

Other referral agency 1-800-Lifenet

Early Intervention Prevention Hotline   1-800-577-2229
Alcoholics Anonymous   212-219-5380   1-800-444-1014
Narcotics Anonymous   212-929-6262   1-800-522-5353

Chapter 6

OUT IN THE COLD

Documenting every single item is a very tedious, time consuming, monotonous task. What if you didn't document anything? What if you didn't keep documentation? You never reported anything. You hoped it would all just go away. You have endured months, if not years, of harassment and now you are put on the defense. You could have lost your cool after being repeatedly "pushed." You could very well have been physically attacked in your workplace and now you are the one being terminated. Anything is possible. You are being fired and left out in the cold. You compiled none or very little documentation; therefore, any litigation would be difficult if not impossible.

The best thing for you to do is probably just go on with your life. You may be experiencing extreme difficulty during this time, while you seek to obtain some justice. If that is the case then here you go. Remember keep it 100% legal. Do not do anything illegal to get satisfaction. Never take revenge, seek vengeance, or in any way sabotage your now ex-employer. You do not want to find yourself on the wrong side of the law. There are hundreds of agencies, which you can contact. You will be able to get help and justice, all legally.

Every company has secrets. Expose them, find them out and expose them. If you are fired, terminated from the company without any severance package whatsoever, left out in the cold, face it. The company you have devoted a majority of your life to has ceased any loyalty towards you. It is now time for you to do the same. Do not expose the company's marketing policies, business procedures, or any other confidential business-oriented material. That would constitute sabotage. You could possibly be held accountable for any revenues lost by your ex-employer. Instead expose the secrets of any wrong doings, any illegalities. If a business practice happens to be illegal, then expose it.

Does the company that unjustly constructively discharged you comply with all laws regarding the hiring of minorities? For instance, you noticed that there are way too few African-Americans represented in your ex-workplace. There may be a few African-American individuals scattered throughout the company to be used as tokens. That is a secret of the company's that can be exposed to the EEOC, NAACP, local civil rights and community leaders, etc... Any number of repercussions can occur, from nothing being done at all to maybe a full blown demonstration, demanding fair treatment in hiring practices, outside your ex-employer. Maybe even the media might show up with live cameras on the demonstration, all legal.

Is the building, where the company is at, up to building codes? Is it able to pass inspection? Is it free of asbestos? Lead-paint? Are the chemicals used in the company stored properly? Are there adequate fire exits? Are they clear of clutter? Etc., if not contact OSHA, local building inspectors, fire inspector, and local health inspectors. All this could lead to very costly fines and in some cases the redesigning of your ex-company. The company must comply with whatever the inspectors deem necessary. A wall may possibly be needed to be removed to put in a fire exit, or any number of other repercussions from the inspection may occur. You will be creating a safer working environment for your ex-coworkers (a few bad apples didn't spoil the whole bunch). Plus you ensured that no one in the future will ever have to experience the illegalities and infractions that you were forced to endure.

Are all the taxes being paid in your ex-company? All taxes, taxes on sales, taxes from employees' wages, employees being paid cash, etc., If there is any sign of any tax illegalities contact these three agencies: first the IRS, then your state's tax office, and then your city's tax office. A thorough audit of your ex-company by federal, state and local agents should discover any tax fraud illegalities.

Does your ex-employer comply with local recycling laws? Is there separating of plastic, glass, newspaper, cardboard, tin, white computer/copy papers or is every thing just thrown out? Contact your city's Department of Sanitation and the Environmental Protection Agency. (EPA)

Are people with disabilities treated fairly? Was there even one wheelchair-bound person working there? Can someone with a wheelchair or crutches even get in the employee entrance? Are the elevators large enough? Or is the place "stairs only"?

Contact the People with Disabilities federal and state offices. You will be doing the right thing in helping people with disabilities now and in the future.

Is your ex-employer a restaurant? Do all the employees have their green cards? Is liquor served? Does the restaurant comply with the state's liquor law? Does the restaurant or bar follow correct carding procedures for their young guest? If the answer is no to any of these questions contact the appropriate agencies including the Department of Immigration and/or the State Liquor Authority, in addition to the offices already stated (OSHA, Labor, Sanitation, Health Department, minorities, disabilities, etc., whatever the particulars may happen to be).

The possibilities are endless to the numerous outside agencies that are available for you to contact. Just remember, keep it legal. Never lie when filing a complaint. Never exaggerate any incident. Make completely sure that any complaint that you ever file is 100% accurate before you sign it. If you fabricate an event you can be jailed.

If you claim that your ex-company is racist and you file federal charged with the EEOC, there better be signs of racism throughout the place when EEOC gets there to investigate. If you claim the working conditions are unsafe and not up to standard, they better be that way when the federal, state, and city inspectors do finally find the time to get in there to inspect.

Contacting outside agencies for assistance will prove to be very therapeutic. The more you talk about it the sooner you will be able to get over it and continue on with your life. You will be getting to talk to someone who is able to remain objective simply because they are not receiving a paycheck from the company that you are filing allegations against. Only a person working within a particular company knows of its many secrets. In each case the secrets and the outcome would be completely different. The secrets do not have to expose only illegalities. Secrets of an unethical and/or immoral nature can be freely exposed, just make sure you do not overstep that sabotage boundary.

You will be doing an extensive amount of letter writing to all these agencies. Make copies of every letter you write before you send it out. Every agency you contact by mail should contact you back by mail. If you do not receive a correspondence follow up the letter with a phone call. You want to get a return letter of each and every outside agency that you contact. You want to see in writing what the agency's response and course of action is.

Approaching outside agencies for help and some answers should put you on the path to getting over it all and moving on. If you are still upset after all this, you can then turn to the media. Be forewarned though, depending on the nature of the information you disclose to the press, you can very well be thrust into a fifteen minutes of fame media frenzy that you could not possibly be prepared for or want.

Congratulations. You were able to keep your head during turbulent times. You didn't return to the ex-workplace and create massive bloodshed. That alone is enough to earn you ex-employee of the month, or at least some recognition after the way they treated you. You kept it 100% legal. You merely exposed a few illegalities that should not be in a professional working environment in the first place. You have now reached closure. You can now move on peacefully with your life.

To recap chapter 6

You have been fired and left out in the cold, after years of loyal service with no severance package, and you want justice or even satisfaction at this point. Expose any and all illegalities and embarrassing secrets. Keep it legal and free of revenge, sabotage, or vengeance of any kind.

ADDITIONAL LISTINGS

Your goal has now become addressing and exposing any and all illegalities in your ex-workplace. Contact these agencies.

DEPARTMENT OF SANITATION /EPA

Sanitation Police	718-714-2731
Sanitation Complaints	212-219-8090
Environmental Protection Agency	718-595-5595
EPA (state)	718-482-4949
EPA (federal)	212-637-3000
EPA (headquarters)	202-260-2090

Council on The Environment of NYC
51 Chambers Street
New York, N.Y.
212-788-7900

HEALTH DEPARTMENTS

NYC Health Department Complaints 212-442-1999
NYC H. D. Restaurant Inspections   212-442-9666
Crisis Hotline   1-800-527-7474
NY State Dept. of Health   212-268-7185

TAX AGENCIES

Tax evasion hotline   718-403-4310
NYC Comptroller–Alan Hevesi (D)   212-669-3500
NYS Comptroller–H. Carl McCall (D) 212-681-4489
NYS Comptroller–Executive offices   212-681-4482
State Department of Taxation   1-800-225-5829
Internal Revenue Service   1-800-829-1040

FIRE PREVENTION

New York State Office of Fire Prevention & Control   518-474-6746
New York City Prevention–Complaints, Violations   718-999-2541
Headquarters Inspections Unit   718-999-2476

BUILDING REGULATIONS

New York City Department of Building   212-312-8000
60 Hudson Street   212-312-8531
N.Y.,N.Y. 10013
Customer Service   212-312-8904
Complaints   212-312-8530 or 212-312-8750
Asbestos Complaints   1-800-368-5888 or 718-403-1300
24-Hour Hotline   718-337-4357

INSPECTOR GENERAL   212-788-8010
Investigating Department   212-825-5900
Information–N.Y. State Agency   212-417-4000

STATE LIQUOR AUTHORITY (SLA)

Research your own states
SLA in New York State, call 212-417-4002
11 Park Place
New York, N.Y. 10007

IMMIGRATION ISSUES

Immigration & Naturalization   1-800-375-5283
Immigration & Naturalization   212-206-6500
Immigration Enforcement   212-264-5924
Immigrant Affairs   212-788-7654
Office of the Mayor
N.Y, N.Y. 10007

MEDIA SOURCES

New York Daily News	212-210-2100
New York Post	212-930-8000
New York Times	212-556-1234
New York Newsday	212-251-6600
USA Today	212-715-5350
Village Voice	212-475-3300
AP	212-621-1500
UPI	212-560-1100

TELEVISION–ALL (212)

New York One	465-0111
CBS	975-4321
NBC	664-4444
FOX	452-5555
ABC	456-7777
CNN	714-7800
WPIX	949-1100
ABC Hotline	1-877-TIP-NEWS
	847-6397

Chapter 7

WHAT EVERY MANAGER SHOULD KNOW

Every single m/s/b should have employee relations train-ing regardless if they are in a supervisory position or not. If you are ever hired, promoted, assigned, or placed in a posi-tion in which you supervise, manage, or in any other way oversee employees you MUST be trained in that area. There is such a shortage of qualified m/s/b(s) that companies will hire virtually anyone, with no formal education or training, to fill these crucial positions.

Case in point, a restaurant for instance. The m/s/b has to work an average of 60 hours per week. He must pur-chase his own business attire. He must be there first thing in the morning to unlock the door. At night he is the last one out the door after all the servers have banked out and the place is spotless. Then he sets the alarm. He is lucky to take home $500 a week after all that. The server on the other hand works an average of 40 hours a week, has their uniform supplied to them, and gets to leave after their work is done. They take home about $700 a week. Any stressful situations that happen throughout the course of the day are directed immediately toward the m/s/b. It is no wonder why there is a shortage of qualified m/s/b(s).

Two local business owners were having coffee one morning. One says, "It sure is hard to find good help, nowa-days." The other one responded, "Good help?!!! You can't even find bad help these days."

Employees are the backbone of every company, with-out them you cannot possibly operate a business. A very important part in employee relations is motivation. How do you keep an employee motivated and continually hard work-ing? There are numerous theories on the subject of motiva-tion. A few of these theories are based on the "needs met" concept. The concept has become so popular that many anger management programs have incorporated the needs met idea extensively. It is up to you, the m/s/b, if you are in a supervisory position to research the needs met concept and become familiar with it.

WHAT CAN YOU CONTINUALLY DO AS A MANAGER, SUPERVISOR OR BOSS TO DISSIPATE ANY POTENTIAL WORKPLACE VIOLENCE IN YOUR COMPANY?

1. Ensure all lines of communication are open.
2. Listen and respond.
3. Take action.

Ensure all lines of communication are open. Violence has a chance to occur when frustration sets in and frustration sets in when communications break down. An employee should be able to turn to any m/s/b for any reason at any time during their employment. No m/s/b should be off limits or unapproachable. An employee may not feel comfortable reporting directly to their immediate supervisor. You as a m/s/b must keep the lines of communications open. Regardless if you are an entry-level m/s/b or the top m/s/b, it is up to you to ensure that all lines of communication are kept open. A few effective ideas might be an open door policy, a suggestion box (check it every day, don't let dust accumulate on it), or maybe set up a direct hotline to the general manager or top person in charge. Whatever works in your company, as long as it works, and all lines of communications are kept open.

Listen and respond. There will come a day in your career that an employee will approach you with a situation. It will be up to you to meet the employee's needs, so that the employee can move on from the situation and continue being the productive employee that they are. You must realize that before this employee has approached you, he has thought it over repeatedly and probably dreads coming forward. It is taking him a tremendous amount of courage to address this situation.

He needs to speak to you. He also needs privacy and your complete undivided attention. You have got to meet these needs by providing a private office where you both can sit down. You have got to give him at least 10 minutes of your undivided attention to just listen to his situation.

SYMPATHY – BEEN THERE, DID THAT

EMPATHY – HAVEN'T BEEN THERE, CAN UNDERSTAND THAT

Sympathy refers to the mutual understanding of one's feelings, a shared affection for the distress of another, compassion.

Empathy refers to the understanding of another person's feelings.

Sympathy – People who have had the same exact experiences, mutual understanding, shared affection, been there did that.

Empathy – Understanding of another person's feelings. Although you may not agree with another persons' feelings or may not have had the same experience yourself you are capable of understanding the feelings of another human being. Haven't been there, can understand that.

For example, you have a dog that is 14 years old. One day the dog dies. You are sad, you grieve, and you move on. Years later a friend of yours, dog happens to die. He is sad. You have sympathy for your friend, a shared affection (his dog died, your dog died), a mutual understanding for his distress. Been there, did that.

Now empathy, same example. You have had your dog 14 years now and you love him very much, he is 98 in dog years. Your friend's dog happens to die. You now feel empathy for your friend, an understanding of feelings, for his devastating loss. You could imagine how sad you would feel if your dog were to die. You have not personally had the same experience, in this case, of the pet dog dying (just wait), but you can understand the feeling. Haven't been there, can understand that.

You cannot be both sympathetic and empathetic at the same time on the same subject. Either you have been there (sympathetic) or you haven't (empathetic). While you are meeting this employee's needs, you must listen with a sympathetic or an empathetic ear, whatever the case may be and remain non-judgmental. A person may not be crying hysterically in front of you but that does not mean they aren't shattered inside.

You need to be using this time effectively by listening and gathering facts. During the meeting, after the employee has had ample time to say whatever it is he is feeling, you must inform him of your course of action. You will need to act on the situation. End the meeting by informing him that you will get back to him in a timely manner after you have had a chance to investigate the situation. Anything longer than 72 hours is unacceptable.

You as the m/s/b/ must now act on the situation for two reasons: first the employee is awaiting your response. You told him you would get back to him; you can't leave him hanging now. You must meet his needs. Second, if the employee happened to show up at the meeting with a stack of proper documentation, spoke rationally, concisely, and you sensed that he knows what he is doing, is experienced, or maybe has even read a copy of this book, you better believe he has documented the meeting that the two of you just had. He probably included minute details, your reaction, your response, your stated course of action, your actual course of action, or lack of, etc.

Cover yourself. If you ignore or fail to follow up with this employee, or if the situation isn't resolved, you can be sure this employee will be going to your immediate supervisor at some point in the near future. You are the one who could be facing questions like "Why hasn't this situation been taken care of long ago?" "What have you done about this?" It is very important that the m/s/b meets the needs of the employee and rectifies any situation before it has a chance to escalate to a huge problem.

Take action. Most corporations have empowerment programs. Empower yourself to benefit the employee. Become familiar with the needs met concept. Look around to see what can be done in your particular company. What changes can you make? Does your company have mental coverage? It is a thing of the present. It will become a standard part of every companies benefit package in the twenty-first century. If your company does not offer mental health benefits take action and do something about it. There is always some action you can take. Safer working conditions, employee relations, rectifying any areas where minorities are misrepresented, etc. No company is 100% perfect. There will always be something you can do to better the working environment at your company. Take any action necessary to create a violence-free workplace.

Currently there are numerous labor laws and more are being added constantly. There are federal, state, city, and local municipality laws. There are sexual harassment laws, civil rights laws, gay right laws, environmental laws, and disability laws – the list is endless. You must keep abreast of them not only to protect the company you work for, but also to protect yourself against any costly litigation.

Laws change so rapidly that there is no way possible to keep up with all of them while still doing your job. Set aside time to sit down and dissect the new laws to make sure their meaning is completely clear and concise. M/s/b's should be made to attend a weeklong seminar on current employment law changes and employee relations every three to five years.

There might be a time in your career where you may actually have a bonafide problem employee. You have no choice but to move for this person's termination. You must make sure you do it legally. You must follow your company's particular procedures. It would be very safe to assume that the employee has a copy of the company's policies. You must have a file consisting of a series of well-documented disciplinary problems in the past against this employee. This file must include any and all counseling sessions, verbal warning, written warning, suspension, and any disciplinary actions whatsoever, any written statements by other employees; every shred of evidence you have, against this employee, must be in this file.

It is very important that you do everything legal as not to violate this person's basic rights. This person may very well be a problem employee that really needs to be fired, but if you do not follow your company's procedures and policies or worse break any employment laws in terminating this person, you and the company you work for can be facing an embarrassing lawsuit.

You may be faced with the decision to terminate an employee throughout your career. You can only do this after you have afforded this individual each and every opportunity possible. You should attempt to make the transition as smooth as possible. If you have any inclination that there may be trouble ahead try to avoid it immediately. A settlement should be considered especially if you sense this employee will fight it or if this employee seems experienced with stacks of proper documentation. (You must realize also that this is only the documentation that they are showing you.) Settle if this person seems to you to be crazy, psychotic, disgruntled, or capable of returning to the workplace to commit mass violence. A small settlement is nothing compared to the possibility of numerous wrongful death lawsuits the company potentially faces if the catastrophe were to actually take place. Plus the tragedy would attract negative media coverage.

A year's pay should be an adequate amount. It is worth

it for the company to pay out $40,000 now and be done with it. You could fight it and drag it out for months, years even, and try to wear down the ex-employee. He can wear you and other current employees down in the process also, therefore hindering the company's potential productivity. If the person is a true DisGruntled Employee the rage they are feeling can keep them motivated to fight for years. Do you really want or need that? Corporate lawyers get $200 per hour minimum. Multiply that times six months. Even after spending all that money, there still could be no resolution. The ex-employee feels that he has been wronged and he has nothing to lose at this point.

The company has fired him. There is nothing to stop him now from going to the media with any of the company's secrets or exposing anything that he wants.

You may spend anywhere from thousands to millions on your public relations campaign, depending upon the size of your company. Isn't it worth it to protect it, by offering a mere year's salary? This person can just start wreaking all sorts of legal havoc on the company. He can contact any number of governmental agencies: IRS, OSHA, EEOC, ACLU, NYCLU, ADA, DEP, Department of Labor, Sanitation, Health, etc.

This could lead to big fines on the federal level and more importantly it then becomes a matter of public record. He can go on a legal rampage, contacting agencies galore, civil rights leaders, gay rights leaders, fire code officials, building code officials, etc. He can possibly report any minor violation that he may have noted while working as an employee.

This book recommends a quick quiet settlement. You must, as a m/s/b, remain objective and extremely professional. During the termination process this employee very well may have said some nasty things, swore at you, cursed you, raised his voice, threatened litigation, etc. Whatever the case, being fired is an extremely traumatic event.

If there is a chance for a settlement do not let your ego or pride get in the way. You cannot think "Forget him, we're not giving him a damn thing after all that he put us through." You must remain objective and realize what the best thing for the company is. You could be thinking, "It is hard to believe that there was an ex-employee with a questionable work history, who got fired, cursed me out on his way out the door and now he is getting a year's salary to just go away. It is just unbelievable." This could very well be the biggest test of professionalism that you may ever encounter in your career. Remember the best thing for the company is making this person quietly disappear.

A quick settlement would be in everybody's best interest. Or you can proceed with the costly litigation, possible media coverage, and possible inspections from numerous governmental agencies, etc. At this point you know what he has access to.

You do have the upper hand in offering the settlement though, because after all you are the one who has the money. You can have the settlement filled with legal clauses on the side of the company. The company's lawyer should take care of all this. The legal clauses that should be included in a settlement contract are the obvious: a settlement means no further legal action whatsoever. More importantly a silence clause: the employee can never speak to any media agency be it TV, magazine, newspaper, radio, etc. There will be no book deal, no made for TV movie, no play, no comedy skits or stand-up routines, no talking with the friends about it, nothing, 100% silence. If the ex-employee breaks the contract in any manner each and all monies must be returned immediately. This will ensure his silence.

The book cannot overemphasize the need to settle. It will be a mere pittance compared to the legal fees, and possible fines, and public relations nightmare that a

DisGruntled Employee can cause. You, as the manager, have the defining decision on whether or not to settle with this employee. You can take the gamble and hope this person will just go away quietly. The following is an example of a company that took just that chance.

A detective agency, in a wealthy Connecticut community, happened to employ a DisGruntled Employee. An innocent 15-year-old girl was murdered in this same community. Rumors about the murder were flying about in this exclusive gated area. An elder, high-power, old money gentleman happened to hire this certain detective agency. He wanted the detective agency to clear his family's name once and for all, especially that of his two sons. The detective agency conducted their investigation and reported back to the gentleman. Their findings were that his younger son had in fact committed the murder of their neighbor.

This information sat in the detective agency's files for years. One day the DisGruntled Employee, of this detective agency, leaked this information which caused a nationwide media frenzy. That younger son happened to be Michael Skakel and the neighbor was Marsha Moxley. The actions of one DisGruntled Employee resulted in the arrest of a Kennedy family member. The detective agency received enormous publicity. Their reputation and credibility had been severely damaged. Current clients became worried about their own privacy issues and the negative attention did not bring in any new business.

To recap chapter 7

In addition to initial procedures, covered in chapter one, there are on-going, continuing procedures that need to be followed to dispel any potential workplace violence. If you are a m/s/b, enroll yourself in some sort of employee relation class. Ensure all lines of communication are kept open. Listen and respond. Take action. Become familiar with the needs met concept. Learn the latest labor laws. Lastly, settle and settle immediately when it becomes clear that the problem employee is not just going to go away quietly. The damage a DisGruntled Employee can administer will be irreversible.

REFERENCE RESOURCES

APBNEWS.COM, AMW.COM, USATODAY.COM,
OSHA.GOV, SEATTLETIMES.COM,
Honolulu's STARBULLETIN.COM

VARIOUS LAW ENFORCEMENT AGENCIES WEB SITES

DEPARTMENT OF LABOR PUBLICATIONS

NEW YORK PUBLIC LIBRARY REFERENCE CENTER

KEY WEST PUBLIC LIBRARY REFERENCE CENTER

BELL ATLANTIC WHITE PAGES

THE PER ANNUM-MANHATTAN DIARY

NUMEROUS CORPORATIONS' EMPLOYEE HANDBOOKS

ADDITIONAL RECOMMENDED READING

ABRAHAM MAZLOW'S *HIERARCHY OF NEEDS THEORY*